FINDING YOUR GERMAN ANCESTORS

by Dr. Ronald M. Smelser

P.O. Box 476
Salt Lake City, UT 84110

Smelser, Ronald M., 1932–
    Finding your German ancestors / by Ronald M. Smelser.
        p.   cm.
    ISBN 0-916489-51-5
    1. German Americans--Genealogy--Handbooks, manuals, etc.
    2. Germany--Genealogy--Handbooks, manuals, etc.   I. Title.
    E184.G3S64 1991
    929'. 1'08931--dc20   91-8562

Robert J. Welsh, managing editor
Design and production, Robb Barr

First printing 1990
10 9 8 7 6 5 4 3 2 1
Printed in the United States of America

Contents

List of Illustrations

Preface

The text of this guide was written in early 1990 prior to the dramatic and unexpected reunification of Germany. Much has changed since then and further changes are underway. Repositories once split between West and East Germany will be coalesced and often moved to different cities. Many street names in what was East Germany have been or will be changed. We will keep abreast of these developments and will incorporate them in the next edition of the guide. In the meantime, we must assume that mail directed to institutions mentioned in the appendixes of this guide will be forwarded.

Before You Begin. . . .

This brief booklet is designed to be an introduction to the opportunities and problems of finding genealogical sources located in Germany on your German ancestors. It assumes that you have already undertaken a search in the United States to identify your ancestor(s) and have some idea of from where in Germany they may have come. This search would have involved a variety of sources including family Bibles, vital records, church records, passenger lists, diaries, letters, applications for citizenship, and veterans and widows pension applications.

Once you have narrowed down your search to a particular state or area of Germany, this booklet will then introduce you to the available sources.

You should be aware of some of the pitfalls in getting to this point. For example, very often the records are vague as to point of origin. Some simply say "Germany"; other times they give the state of origin such as Prussia or Bavaria. Fortunate is the researcher who finds the actual town or village of origin of his ancestor. Another problem is the matter of spelling. We are used to spelling our names consistently; our ancestors, often illiterate or semi-literate, were not. "Hiedler" would often be rendered as "Hüttler" or some other variation because, pronounced in German, they sound virtually the same. Often names were anglicized upon arrival in this country so that "Schmidt" became "Smith," "Schmeltzer" became "Smelser," or a "Schneider" became "Taylor," a literal translation of the occupation of the person.

Finding our German ancestors represents a great opportunity, but it is also a daunting challenge, perhaps even more daunting than that of our neighbors who are seeking English or French ancestors. This is because of the unique nature of German history, which throws a number of roadblocks in our way.

Three German Traditions

German history is characterized by political fragmentation, religious diversity, and social and military strife, all of which have consequences for the records that we seek. Unlike England or France, which were united as nation states in the late middle ages with highly centralized governments preserving central records and a national capital for focus, Germany remained for centuries a highly heterogeneous nation with a plenitude of political units. There was no such thing as a German nation-state until 1871. As a result, Germany had three traditions that existed side by side: imperial, national, and regional/local.

Although there were powerful German dynasties during the middle ages—Hohenstaufen, Salier—none succeeded in establishing a German nation-state because they were bound by an older, imperial tradition—that of the Roman Empire. Germanic tribes infiltrated and eventually overcame the old Roman Empire. Germans were bound for centuries to the legacy of ancient Rome. Since the ninth century, German kings and emperors aspired to be crowned emperors of what came to be called the Holy Roman Empire of the German Nation. German kings found themselves leading endless campaigns over the Alps to the northern Italian plains in order to keep control of Rome. And when the cat's away the mice will play.

In the absence of the kings, local and regional nobles established their own autonomy and sovereignty, exercising firm control over their own states. Thus, there arose a powerful second tradition in German history, something the Germans call *Kleinstaaterei* or the multiplicity of small states. Both of these traditions, the umbrella tradition of empire and the local tradition of small states, lasted for a thousand years or more as the two most powerful political legacies of the middle ages in Germany.

Ironically, the national tradition that has been strongest for the last two hundred years, was for centuries the weakest, often only a dream in the minds of visionaries. There was a strong national cultural tradition but not a political one. Only the modern era and French invasions would awaken it—just in time for the mass migration of Germans in the nineteenth century. Considering all of German history then, political fragmentation was predominately the norm.

Exacerbating these conflicting traditions in Germany was the religious strife that dominated central Europe during the sixteenth and seventeenth centuries and provided the backdrop for the first wave of German immigration to our shores. The Reformation, the revolt of Protestants against the Catholic church, really began in Germany with Martin Luther. The Reformation resulted in a plethora of new religious denominations and sects, including Lutherans, Anabaptists, Pietists, and others, as well as prolonged and bloody warfare amongst the Great Powers, largely carried out on German soil. This warfare culminated in the Thirty Years War (1618-48), which decimated large parts of Germany, killed nearly one third of the population, and of course destroyed precious records sadly missed in our genealogical research today.

Eventually the war ended in an exhausted truce where Catholic and Lutheran princes could decide which religion their respective territories would observe. However, Anabaptists and other sects were not tolerated, and these fled to America after pauses in Bohemia, Holland, England, and other more tolerant parts of Europe. The first wave of immigrants to America was thus religiously inspired and by the late eighteenth century involved over a quarter million people.

The result of centuries of religious strife was more fragmentation in Germany. As the modern era dawned in the late eighteenth century, there were hundreds of sovereign states comprising Germany: 314 states and 1475 estates including imperial knightdoms, imperial free cities, ecclesiastical estates, baronies, electorates, margravates, and so on. The map of Germany resembled a patchwork quilt.

These historic developments have tremendous implications for the genealogist. Huge numbers of records were destroyed. The most useful records for the researcher during this period—from the late 1500s on—are parish registers kept by village clerics, which included information on births, confirmations, marriages, and deaths. Thousands of these registers perished in the conflagration, as did hundreds of thousands of people.

In the Palatinate, for example, from which large numbers of Germans came to America, it is estimated that only 50,000 people of an original population of one million survived the Thirty Years War. Baden lost over half its buildings, leaving thousands to live in caves. Thus, many a promising family tree ends abruptly in the sixteenth or seventeenth century. However, many people soon came from neighboring territories to repopulate these devastated lands—from Switzerland, Alsace-Lorraine, and Bavaria. This in-migration represents an opportunity, because the parish records of these immigrants, largely postdating the religious wars, are more likely to have remained intact.

Another problem resulted from the wars—large segments of German territory came under foreign rule (for example, Alsace under the French and Pomerania under the Swedes). This must be accounted for in the records. Many eighteenth-century Germans who immigrated to America claimed Swedish or French nationality even though they were ethnic Germans.

3

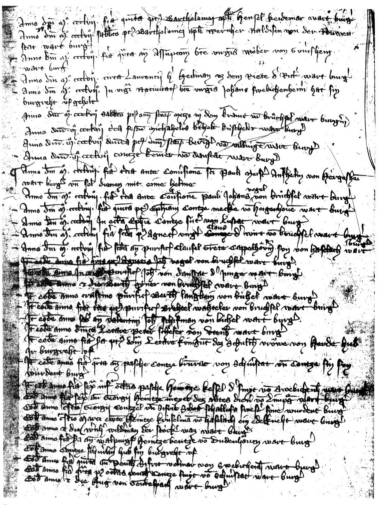

Illustration 1. Speyer Bürgerbuch, citizenship list, 1344.

If one of your ancestors was fortunate enough to be a citizen of a German town in the late Middle Ages, you may be in luck. Few are able to trace their ancestry prior to the destruction of the Reformation religious wars.

4

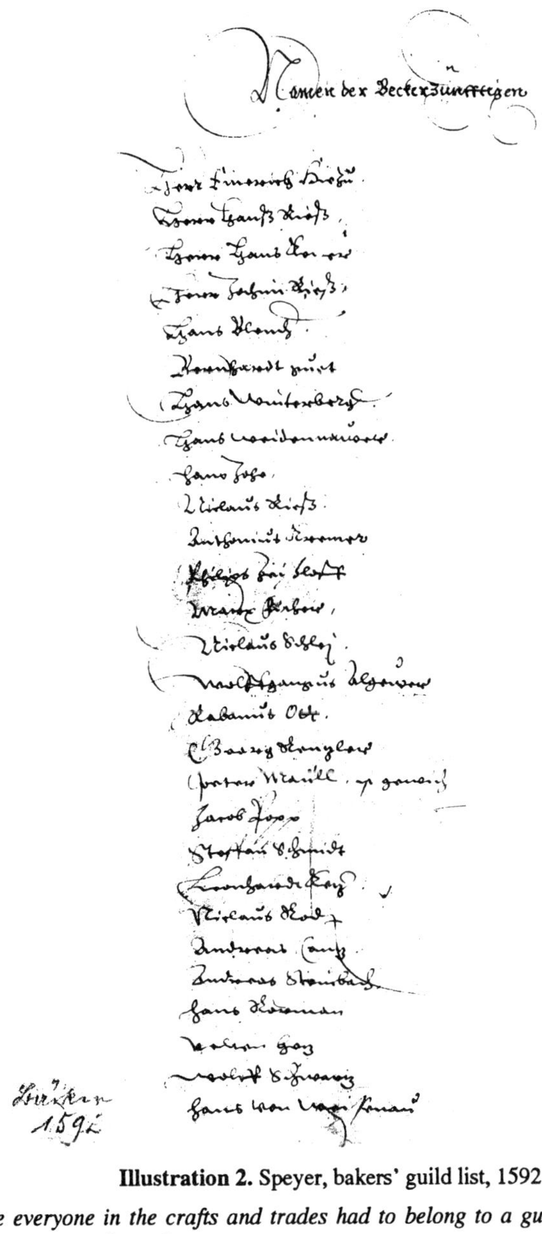

Illustration 2. Speyer, bakers' guild list, 1592.

Since everyone in the crafts and trades had to belong to a guild, these lists are important genealogical sources.

5

Analogous were the Jewish immigrants to America in the early twentieth century who were listed as Russians because of their country of origin.

This first wave of German migration to America came largely from the states of Baden, Württemberg, Bavaria, Hesse, and from the Münster and Mainz regions. In the early eighteenth century, they were joined by people from Swabia and the Palatinate.

As noted, the parish register is often the only, and by far the most important, source in tracing German ancestors. There are other sources as well, particularly if your ancestor came from one of the important free cities like Nuremberg, Augsburg, Speyer, Bremen, Hamburg, or Danzig. These independent cities generated many kinds of records important to the researcher. Records, often extending back to the twelfth and thirteenth century, include citizen lists, muster rolls, charity and hospital records, municipal records, tax rolls, notarial documents, and property rolls. Particularly useful are guild records. At a time when virtually all manufacturing was artisanal cottage industry, every craft organized itself into associations called guilds. These oversaw quality control, fair prices, and the training process from apprentice to journeyman to master. Since the majority of the population was involved, the lists of members in guild records are a valuable source.

Three other sources deserve mention here. Firstly, there are the funeral sermons (*Leichenpridigte*). There are several hundred thousand of these that extend from the mid-sixteenth century to the early 1800s. At the funerals of both the high born and even the many ordinary people, the cleric memorialized that person's life, thus leaving a valuable source for subsequent generations. Secondly, there are the German Lineage Books (*Deutsche Geschlechterbücher*). These are the family trees from middle-class families, usually dating from the eighteenth century. Several hundred have been published to date. Finally, one should mention local family books (*Ortssippenbücher*). These are compilations of family trees on a local level done by German genealogists, some published, some in manuscript form. Most of the above are available in local archives, although some are in private hands.

The Revolutionary Era

The revolutionary era of the late eighteenth century brought basic changes to Germany. A groundswell of revolution hit the European continent, beginning with France in 1789, and eventually spilling over into Germany with the advent of Napoleon and his conquering French armies. The revolutionary era posed a profound threat to the German princes, great and small, and to all that they stood for. The following became threatened:

- absolute princes who received their legitimacy from God and not from the governed

- a feudal system tying people to the land and their landlord making them subjects and not citizens

- an economic system where the state played a primary role

- a rigid class system based on the privileges of the well-born who, among other things, were exempt from taxes

- the power of entrenched church officials

- a provincial orientation

- the regime of tiny states.

But the revolution also meant opportunity: a free enterprise economic system, the primacy of law, civic equality, representative government, and basic civil rights enshrined in a constitution. The Germans began to awaken from the torpor of decades. That awakening would eventually lead, in part, to the second wave of migration to America, which was by far the largest.

In the meantime, the French began to remake the map of Germany, both literally and figuratively. Where French armies came, feudalism and personal servitude were abolished, the guild system was dismantled, liberal economic principles were enshrined, and the metric system was introduced. Also, important for research, a second major kind of documentation was begun: the civil registry of vital records, which would parallel the records of the church from then on. Introduced by the French on the west bank of the Rhine in 1798, these civil registers gradually spread to other parts of Germany—to Baden in 1810, to Frankfurt in 1850, and to the kingdom of Prussia in 1864. In 1876 they were introduced in all parts of the newly unified German Empire.

The French also greatly simplified the map of Germany. By 1806 the venerable but moribund Holy Roman Empire had been disbanded. The vast majority of tiny states and estates also disappeared from the map, their territory absorbed by larger states. The French also "promoted" some states under their control. Bavaria and Württemberg were elevated to kingdoms; Baden and Hesse-Darmstadt were elevated to grand duchies.

As the power of the lesser princes eroded, many were recompensed for their losses. Some of their territory was kept as private property. They also

7

kept their archives, with records important for the researcher. Many of these archives were absorbed by state archives in the twentieth century; many still remain in the castles where they originally resided and are considered private property.

The outcome of all these changes imposed by the French greatly weakened the local and imperial traditions that had for so long dominated German history. The Holy Roman Empire and large numbers of tiny states had disappeared. The German national tradition, long relegated to the realm of culture, was born politically. Beginning in the early years of the nineteenth century, the German national tradition would grow to become a most powerful political force in Germany, ironically at just the time when unprecedented numbers of Germans would leave their fatherland.

In 1815, Napoleon was defeated and a provisional political system was put into place on German territory. It was not yet a German nation state, but it was not a return to the past either. Rather, an awkward compromise between past and future ensued. Germany now consisted of thirty-nine sovereign states loosely organized into a Germanic Confederation dominated by Austria. The states were sovereign, and the only real institution of the confederation was a diet, or assembly, which met in Frankfurt and to which each state sent representatives. (A small map on page 14 shows these sovereign states from which many nineteenth-century ancestors came.) In most of these states, relieved princes tried to restore much of their old authority but could not turn back the clock entirely. Some of the states actually granted constitutions, such as the Duchy of Nassau in 1814; Saxe-Weimar in 1816; and Bavaria, Baden, and Württemberg in 1818-19.

As time went by, however, the political system established after 1815 proved less and less viable. The forces of economic liberalism, which represented the industrial revolution as well as nationalistic desire for a united Germany, gathered strength. By the 1840s these forces mounted a major challenge to the old authorities. Even the thirty-nine states changed. Several smaller principalities like Hohenzollern-Sigmaringen and Hohenzollern-Hechingen were absorbed by Prussia. The houses of Saxe-Gotha and Hesse-Hamburg died out. These changes also have ramifications for researchers. Eventually, the tiny states and their records and archives were absorbed by the dominant state of Prussia. Today, the records that have survived two world wars reside for the most part in regional and local state and municipal archives.

Mass Migration Begins

It was during the years described at the end of the last section that the great mass migration of Germans to America (and elsewhere) occurred. Immigration had dried up to a trickle during the twenty-five years of revolution and war between 1789 and 1815, largely because of British blockade of the continent. After 1815 immigration picked up again, at first tentatively, then in the 1820s and 1830s in a mounting crescendo. The wave crested in the late 1840s and early 1850s with the peak years being 1847 and 1854. During the 1860s, the wave abated due to both the American Civil War and the wars of German unification. Again in the 1870s, immigration picked up and crested a second time in the 1880s. By the 1890s the new Germany had become a prosperous industrial society that could absorb all its citizens into its economy, causing immigration to slow to a trickle.

What precipitated this nineteenth-century wave of out-migration? Basically there were three factors:

1. Basic structural changes in the economy, concerned mainly with the coming of the industrial revolution to Germany, drove millions to leave.
2. Periodic severe economic downturns due to crop failures and panics exacerbated the impact of the structural changes, causing more to leave.
3. Unlike in the earlier period when German states tried to prevent migration, in the nineteenth century most rulers, fearful of social revolution from below, actually encouraged it.

Although some individuals left Germany for political, religious, or other reasons of conscience, the vast majority left for economic reasons, which were closely linked to the early stages of German industrialization during the 1820s and 1830s. A number of events punctuated the process of industrialization.

The Krupp family, later famous as Germany's arms manufacturers, opened their enterprise in the Ruhr area in the late 1820s. In 1834 various German states came together to form the Zollverein, a customs union that foreshadowed political union almost four decades later. The first railroad tracks were laid in 1835 connecting Nuremberg with Fürth. These events presaged eventual progress but initially produced severe dislocation.

Mass manufacturing cut deeply into the ranks of artisans still organized into guilds. Many saw their livelihoods vanish as their skills became

Illustration 3. Württemberg, application for permission to emigrate, 1788.
Prior to the nineteenth century most states were reluctant to let their people go. These requests were not always honored. Most people were still leaving Germany for religious reasons at this time.

superfluous. Fewer and fewer apprentices and journeymen could expect to be accepted into the ranks of the masters. Indeed, many faced the prospect of becoming wage earners in the new factory system, which meant loss of independence and lower social prestige.

In rural areas, those who had for decades combined small-scale farming with artisanal activities found life suddenly grim. With the growth of industrial centers, there was no longer a need for their small-scale production of cloth, iron, or charcoal, and small farming alone could not support them.

Exacerbating this situation in much of western Germany was the traditional partible form of inheritance (*Realteilungserbrecht*), where the farm had to be divided equally among the children; with the overpopulation of the nineteenth century, the small farms became less and less viable. This system predominated in the Palatinate and southwest Baden. It had also been introduced to Rhine-Hessen and the left bank of the Rhine during French occupation, and the system created a new class of "unlanded" farmers in those areas who had no access to land if they could not inherit. It is no wonder then that so many Germans came from areas where this form of inheritance predominated. In areas like Bavaria, east of the Rhine, where the land was not so divisible (*Anerbenrecht*), holdings were much larger and consequently emigration was smaller.

Add to these structural difficulties the sudden boom and bust periods introduced by early capitalism—frequent depressions and panics accompanied by rapid fluctuations in prices—and one can determine the prime motive for mass migration.

Adding to the bulk of mass migration was the more liberal tendency of most German states in the nineteenth century to let their people go. Earlier, immigrants often had to fight their way out against the will of their rulers. In the nineteenth century, more enlightened state governments saw the advantages in allowing mass migration, using it as a safety valve in revolutionary times. Beginning with Prussia in 1818, followed by Saxony in 1831, most German states bestowed the right to emigrate, although they did try to control the pace of the process.

A public policy on emigration also gave the states the opportunity to protect the emigrants from various kinds of chicanery; by the 1840s migration had become big business. Private groups also got into the act, including the Central Society for German Emigrants (1844) and the National Society (1847). Public policy was so important that it even had an impact on where emigrants went to sail to America.

Prior to the 1830s, most German immigrants went to LeHavre, Antwerp, Rotterdam, or Amsterdam as embarkation points. However, this changed

11

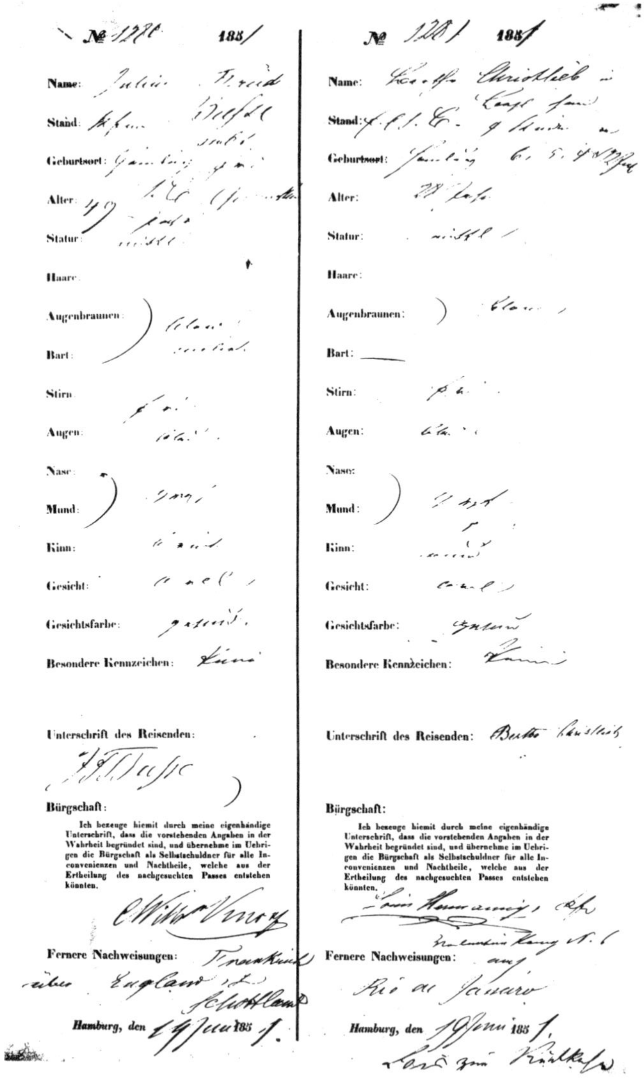

№ 1280 1851

Name:

Stand:

Geburtsort:

Alter: 49

Statur:

Haare:

Augenbraunen:

Bart:

Stirn:

Augen:

Nase:

Mund:

Kinn:

Gesicht:

Gesichtsfarbe:

Besondere Kennzeichen:

Unterschrift des Reisenden:

Bürgschaft:

Ich bezeuge hiemit durch meine eigenhändige Unterschrift, dass die vorstehenden Angaben in der Wahrheit begründet sind, und übernehme im Uebrigen die Bürgschaft als Selbstschuldner für alle Inconvenienzen und Nachtheile, welche aus der Ertheilung des nachgesuchten Passes entstehen könnten.

Fernere Nachweisungen: Frankreich über England u. Schottland

Hamburg, den 19 Juni 1851.

№ 1281 1851

Name:

Stand:

Geburtsort:

Alter:

Statur:

Haare:

Augenbraunen:

Bart:

Stirn:

Augen:

Nase:

Mund:

Kinn:

Gesicht:

Gesichtsfarbe:

Besondere Kennzeichen:

Unterschrift des Reisenden:

Bürgschaft:

Ich bezeuge hiemit durch meine eigenhändige Unterschrift, dass die vorstehenden Angaben in der Wahrheit begründet sind, und übernehme im Uebrigen die Bürgschaft als Selbstschuldner für alle Inconvenienzen und Nachtheile, welche aus der Ertheilung des nachgesuchten Passes entstehen könnten.

Fernere Nachweisungen: Rio de Janeiro

Hamburg, den 19 Juni 1851.

Illustration 4. Hamburg, application for passport, 1851.

Note that these forms give valuable information on a personal level, including size, hair and eye color, shape of face, etc. By the mid-nineteenth century most German states had become much more liberal about permitting emigration. Most people were now leaving for economic reasons.

in the 1830s when the senates of the strategically located port cities of Bremen (1832) and Hamburg (1836) passed laws organizing the "emigrant trade," making the trip quicker and safer and generating a profit at the same time. Consequently, these two ports dominated emigration traffic for the subsequent era of mass emigration after the 1830s.

More active public policy was also important because states pursuing it generated far more records valuable for the researcher than did earlier states. States set up all kinds of procedures or requirements for potential emigrants: taxes had to be paid, debts cleared, and military obligations discharged. Permission had to be secured from various authorities, and all this left a paper trail.

Added to the parish and civil registers, now came an abundance of records reflecting the heightened activities of state bureaucracies concerned with emigration. These included applications for release of citizenship and the actual releases from citizenship, various kinds of passports, applications for permission to emigrate, police permits, settlement of estate and tax matters including expropriation of property for debt payment and lists of debts that emigrants had incurred, records of emigrant property that was sold at auction, and payment of departure taxes.

Some did not leave voluntarily, so there are also records of expulsion proceedings against undesirables as well as records of minor children who were transported at public expense. Proceedings against draft dodgers also are extant. Some immigrants never got very far away from home, largely for financial reasons. Others made it abroad only to die there. There are death certificates for those who died abroad as well as records of returning immigrants.

There are also records reflecting the business of emigration. Contracts abounded with railroads and shipping companies. There are extensive files of emigration agents and private benevolent associations. Massive correspondence also ensued back and forth across the Atlantic. Many newspapers at the time also printed extensive passenger lists as well as samples of immigrant correspondence and search notices for relatives who had immigrated earlier but had since been "lost." The matter of correspondence raises another important area of discussion for the researcher into the past of our German ancestors.

Our viewpoint about the circumstances and patterns of the immigrant's travel has changed considerably in recent years. Earlier studies on immigration to America created the image of lone individuals and nuclear families turning their backs on their past, blindly following their destiny to America, hoping to better their lot, never sure of what they might encounter, while all along the way being cheated by conniving migration agents and venal

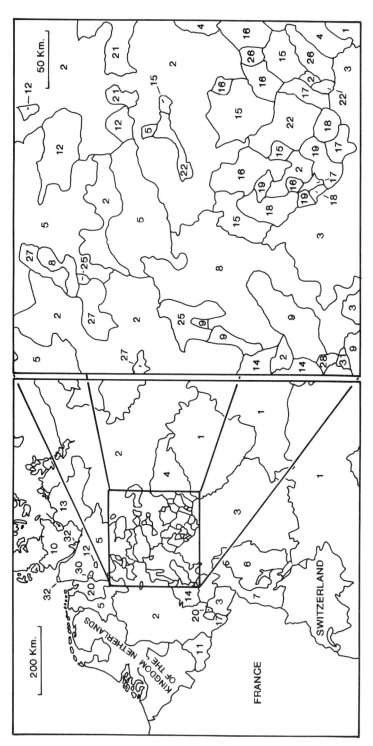

Map of German states during the mass migration of the mid-nineteenth century with map locations (below).

1. Austrian Empire
2. Kingdom of Prussia
3. Kingdom of Bavaria
4. Kingdom of Saxony
5. Kingdom of Hannover
6. Kingdom of Württemberg
7. Grand Duchy of Baden
8. Electorate of Hesse-Kassel
9. Grand Duchy of Hesse-Darmstadt
10. Duchies of Holstein and Lauenburg
11. Grand Duchy of Luxemburg
12. Duchy of Brunswick (Braunschweig)
13. Grand Duchy of Mecklenburg (Schwerin and Strelitz)
14. Duchy and Principality of Nassau, Usingen, and Nassau-Weilburg
15. Grand Duchy of Saxe-Weimar
16. Duchy of Saxe-Gotha
17. Duchy of Saxe-Coburg
18. Duchy of Saxe-Meiningen
19. Duchy of Saxe-Hildburghausen
20. Grand Duchy of Oldenburg
21. Prcipalities of Anhalt (Dessau, Bernburg, and Kothen)
22. Principality of Schwarzburg
23. Principality of Hohenzollern
24. Principality of Lichtenstein
25. Principality of Waldeck
26. Principality of Reuss
27. Principality of Lippe (Schaumburg and Detmold)
28. Principality of Hesse-Homburg
29. Principality of Layen
30. Free City of Bremen
31. Free City of Frankfurt-am-Main
32. Free City of Hamburg
33. Free City of Lübeck

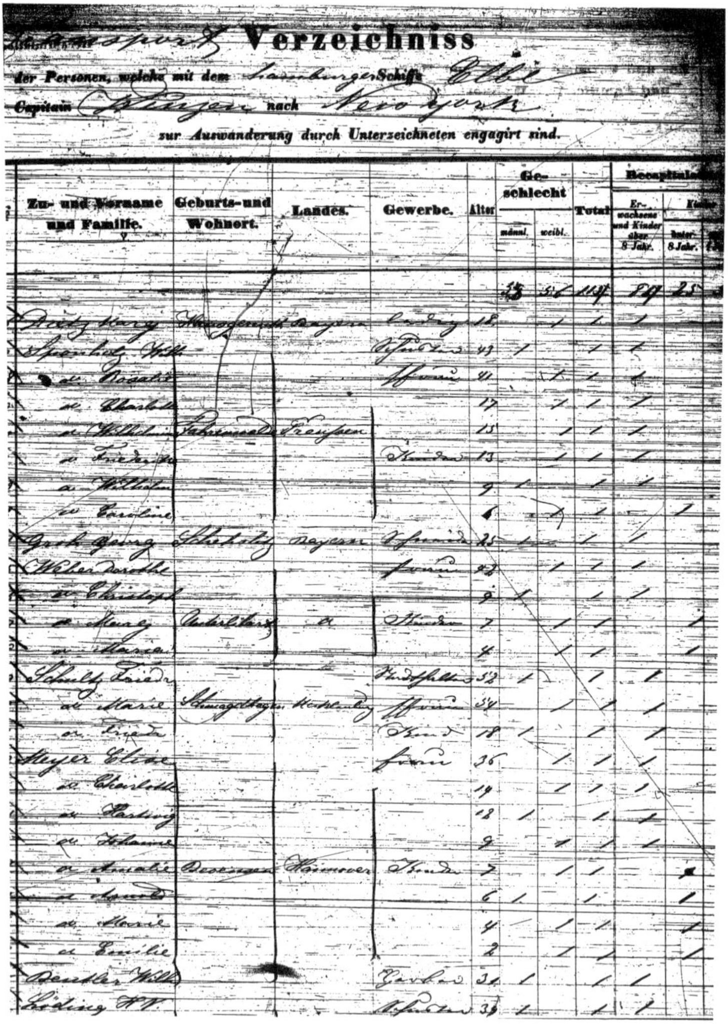

Verzeichniss der Personen, welche mit dem Schiffe Capitain nach zur Auswanderung durch Unterzeichneten engagirt sind.

Zu- und Vorname und Familie.	Geburts- und Wohnort.	Landes.	Gewerbe.	Alter	Geschlecht männl.	Geschlecht weibl.	Total	Recapitulation Erwachsene und Kinder über 8 Jahr.	Kinder unter 8 Jahr.

Illustration 5. Hamburg passenger list, March 1850.

The lists are in chronological order by date of departure. These very valuable lists give the names of millions who departed through Hamburg from 1850 to 1935. Here the ship Elbe, *under Captain Winzen, is sailing to New York.*

officials. The impression is one of disorientation, discontinuity, and credulity. This was an image that corresponded in part to America's image of itself—individualistic, family oriented, pioneer in spirit, cut off from the old world, and possessed of a kind of rude innocence.

But more recent research has revealed a much different picture encompassed in the term "chain migration." It implies a more communitarian effort involving whole villages, parts of villages, or parts of neighboring communities who packed up collectively and came to America where they settled in close proximity to one another and often tried to reshape the old community in the new world. Indeed, they often sought out a landscape similar to the one they had left behind, which can be another important clue for the researcher as to geographic origin.

This form of migration implied a lot more group planning and communication with those still in the old country than the older view. Often, advance teams representing several families came first to assess the environment and report back, or several family members went ahead to stake a claim, then sent for the others.

Letters and people crisscrossed the Atlantic in a far greater pattern of continuity than formerly imagined. Contacts were not so readily severed. This picture also implies much greater knowledge on the part of the immigrants as to what lay ahead. The way was paved, either bureaucratically or by joint exploration.

Perhaps more importantly, the new view underscores the human dignity, autonomy, and ability to make life-changing decisions on the part of our peasant and artisan ancestors. No longer is the image that of the poor and ignorant being acted upon.

It is clear now that these people, as low on the social scale and poor in material resources as they might have been, made their own decision to immigrate, cooperated in organizing the journey, learned intelligently from those who had gone before, and functioned as small communities seeking a better life. Thus, the "chain" was constituted—today it might be called long distance networking—which stretched across three thousand miles and lasted for decades. It is important for the researcher to keep this picture in mind, for exploring its ramifications in the records might help to bridge that often intimidating gulf represented by the Atlantic Ocean.

17

Dorffippenbuch
Kippenheimweiler

Kreis Lahr in Baden

Von

Albert Köbele

und

Pfarrer Erich Henschke

Zeichnungen von Lothar Zierer

Selbstverlag der Verfasser
Grafenhausen und Kippenheim, Kreis Lahr in Baden
1957

Illustration 6.

*On this page and the next page are a cover and a sample page from a "Sippenbuch,"
in this case for the village of Kippenheimweiler in County Lahr, Baden.*

204 ∞ ... 1652: Friedrich Hauβer (aus 203), * an Michaelis 1622, † 6.3.
1680, u. Maria Möllenberg (T.d. Leonhard M., in Münsingen ("Minsingen"), u.d. Susanna geb.Wohlendt.), * um 1637, † 12.12.1683.
6 Kdr· Maria 14.11.1653. - Andreas 28.1.1655, † 5.4.1680. -
Friedrich 20.10.1658, † 11.2.1678. - Anna (838). - Katharina
(461). _ Jakobus 17.5.1666.

H e c k

205 ∞: Johann Michael Heck (S.d. Andreas H., Bürger in Schutterzell, u.
d. Anna Maria geb.Imberin; ∞II s. 206), Bauer und Taglöhner, *Schutterzell (28.9.1754), † Kw 8.8.1815, u. Anna Maria Strahler (aus 840),
* 22.10.1754, † 20.12.1788.
4 Kdr: Michael 10.1.1779, † 20.1.1779. - Andreas 2.11.1781, †.4.
11.1781. - Johannes (207). - Anna Maria (467).

206 ∞ 13.7.1789. Johann Michael Heck (∞I s. 205), u. Juliana Bühler
(T.d. Benedikt B., Hofbauer in Ottoschwanden, u.d. Eva geb.Gerber),
* Ottoschwanden (18.10.1761), † Kw 12.6.1825.
3 Kdr: Johann Michael (208). - Katharina 2.3.1794, † 10.2.1814.
Andreas (209).

207 ∞ 28.11.1809: Johann Heck (aus 205), Wagner, * 13.1.1783, † 5.2.
1814, u. Salome Zipf (aus 1064; s.a. 1078), * 5.7.1788, †7.7.1848.
3 Kdr: Johannes 17.2.1811, † 4.3.1817. - Johann Georg 15.2.13,
† 25.3.1813. - Anna Maria 28.6.1814, ∞ in Mahlberg mit Johann
Schätzle, später nach Amerika ausgewandert.

208 ∞ 1.9.1818: Johann Michael Heck (aus 206), Schmied, * 4.9.1790, †
6.3.1866, u. Maria Elisabetha Mauch (T.d. Michael M., Bauer in Sulz,
u.d. Maria Magdalena geb.Vetter), * um 1796, † 5.8.1850.
7 Kdr: Elisabetha (1091). - Andreas (210). - Friedrich 2.3.1823,
Schmied, nach Amerika ausgewandert. - Johann Georg 4.5.1825, †15.
4.1829. - Johann Michael (211). - Johann Georg 3.8.1830,Schmied,
nach Amerika ausgewandert.

209 ∞ 18.9.1831: Andreas Heck (aus 206), Zimmermann, * 23.11.1799, †
8.12.1882, u. Maria Magdalena Fleig (aus 114), * 23.8.1809, † 16.1.
1850. - 11 Kdr: Knabe †* 1832. - Mädchen †* 1833. - Maria Magdalena (986). - Katharina (212). - Andreas 23.10.1837, † 27.4.
1838. - Anna Maria (1103). - Wilhelm (213). - Friederike (214).
Jakob 16.7.1845, † 12,8,1845. - Andreas 20.10.1847, † 19.1.1927,
Mädchen †* 16.1.1850.

210 ∞ 23.2.1851: Andreas Heck (aus 208), Schmied und Bauer, * 31.1.
1821, † 24.12.1869, u. Magdalena Mauch (T.d. Michael M., Landwirt
in Sulz, u.d. Barbara geb.Mutschler), * Sulz 7.10.1829, † 28.3.
1904. - 7 Kdr: Johann Georg (215). - Knabe †* 29.10.1853. -
Knabe †* 31.10.1854. - Mädchen 7.7.1856, † 8.7.1856. - Knabe †*
10.3.1858. - Friedrich (217). - Andreas (218).

211 ∞ 13.8.1855: Johann Michael Heck (aus 208), Schmied, * 23.11.1828,
† 30.4.1870, u. Katharina Zipf (aus 1086), * 12.11.1829, †16.2.1890.
8 Kdr. Wilhelm 25.2.1854, nach Amerika ausgewandert. - Johann
1.7.1856. - Anna Maria (638). - August 14.9.1860, † 10.12.1932,
led.Arbeiter. - Julius 15.3.1863, nach Amerika ausgewandert. -
Karolina (216). - Maria Magdalena 21.8.1866, ∞ in Karlsruhe. -
Georg 14.4.1869.

212 o-o(1864): Katharina Heck (aus 209), * 5.7.1836.
2 Kdr. Adolf (219). - Katharina 30.4.1874.

213 ∞ 15.1.1871: Wilhelm Heck (aus 209), Landwirt und Taglöhner, * 31.

- 131 -

Illustration 7.

(continued from previous page) *There are hundreds of such books that often provide a shortcut to time-consuming research.*

19

Review of Important Resources

In 1871 Germany was united under the auspices of Prussia, the largest state, into a federal system incorporating twenty-two princely states and three urban republics—Hamburg, Bremen, and Lübeck. This structure lasted until 1918, when, after losing the First World War, Germany lost extensive territories, including Alsace-Lorraine (to France), West Prussia (to Poland), and small bits of territory to Belgium, Denmark, and Czechoslovakia. The Second World War witnessed not only enormous devastation, including records, but also the further loss of territory, including all of the provinces east of the Oder-Neisse rivers (Silesia, Pomerania, East Prussia, and part of Brandenburg), to Poland or to the Soviet Union. What resulted was two Germanies, East and West, each with their own repositories as well as sources in neighboring countries that had annexed former German territory (although most of East Prussia's records were rescued and transported to the West in 1944 and reside in West Germany). Widespread destruction and dramatic population and border shifts in our own century further determine the circumstances under which we do research.

Some of the most important sources available in German archives are also held in the United States at the Family History Library in Salt Lake City. However, as voluminous as the collection there may be, it is incomplete and varies from state to state. In many cases, you will still have to avail yourself of the German archive. Important resources follow:

Church records. For times prior to the nineteenth century these are by far the most common records. Parish registers (*Kirchenbücher*) were mandated by the Catholic church after the Council of Trent (1545–63) and somewhat later by the Protestant churches, although in Baden and Württemberg there are records dating back to 1535. These parish registers recorded baptisms, marriages, and deaths. As time went on, more information was added. By the eighteenth century, for example, marriage records revealed the names of bride and groom, the groom's occupation, his residence, the names of his parents, and often the names of the bride's parents as well. Death records recorded name, occupation, age, and cause of death. Other church records included confirmation, first communion, and occasionally family books in which the priest would give more detailed information on each family including, in the nineteenth century, the notation of immigration abroad.

At the beginning of the nineteenth century, German state governments required for statistical reasons that copies of parish records (*Duplikaten*) be turned over to authorities, thus providing a copy should the original be

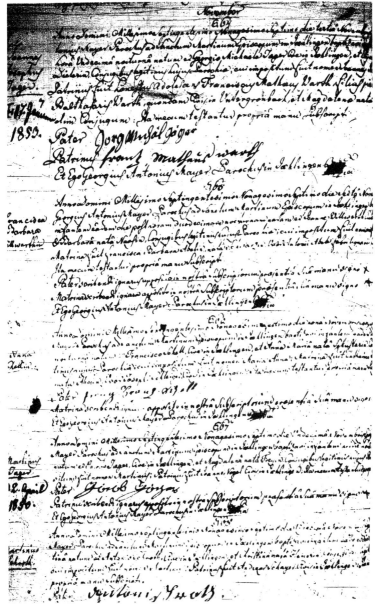

Illustration 8. Jöhlingen, Baden, parish register, November 1797.

By far the most common source prior to modern vital records is the parish register.
Here is a sample page.

missing. This practice was abandoned when civil registers began to be required generally in the 1870s.

There is also valuable material represented in the funeral sermons, German lineage books, and local family books. Though less frequently used, grave registers, church receipt books (*Einnahmebücher*), and separate confirmation books should be noted.

Military records are also important. In this context it should be noted that various military units in garrison towns are listed in military parish registers for that community.

Civil registers. After 1876 these became standard in all parts of the German empire, although they appeared earlier in some of the separate states and were introduced in the Rhineland by the French as early as 1798. Civil registers recorded births, marriages, and deaths.

Guild records. These records, mentioned earlier in the text, are available for a few German towns and cities where artisanal activities were important. They include information on a number of matters involving the guilds, but of greatest interest to the genealogist will be the membership lists, which often included place and date of marriage, and names of wives and children. Unfortunately, for the vast majority of our ancestors who lived as peasants on the land, these records are not pertinent. Other records that, like guild records, are associated generally with towns and cities include tax records, legal records including wills and disposition of property, medical and charity records that recorded the names of those in public or church charge, and citizenship lists. These vary tremendously in availability, but in some cases they go back to the twelfth and thirteenth centuries.

Emigration and immigration records. There are many records from various German states in the nineteenth century concerning migration because the state became very much involved in this process. In this context, passenger lists are an important bridge across the Atlantic. There are various collections of these. By far the most valuable are the Hamburg lists, which record all immigrants going through that port between 1850 and 1934, as well as the Württemberg lists, which record applications to emigrate, mostly in the nineteenth century but in some cases going back much earlier. Both of these lists are available in the Family History Library in Salt Lake City.

Census records. Unlike the United States, which has been a united country since the late eighteenth century and has undertaken a federal

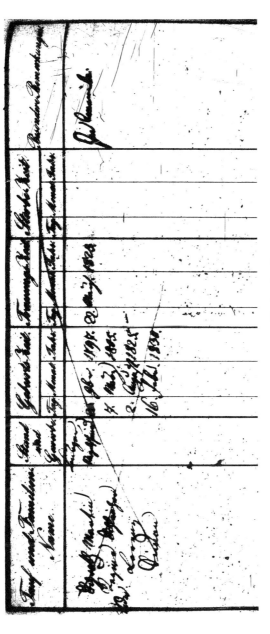

Illustration 9.

Often priests or pastors would also keep information on families in their parish family books (Familienbücher). Here is a sample from the same parish that has a parish register shown in illustration 8. Note that Martinus Schroth, whose birth is noted in the register, reappears later in the family book where he is noted as "in America."

census every ten years since 1790, Germany's political fragmentation prevented such a national undertaking until unification. However, various German states did undertake occasional censuses during the nineteenth century. The availability of such censuses for a given area can be ascertained by writing:

(for West Germany)
>Statistishes Bundesamt
>Postfach 5528
>Gustav Stresemann Ring 11
>6200 Wiesbaden

or

(for East Germany)
>Staatliche Zentralverwaltung für Statistik der DDR
>Hans Beimler Strasse 70-72
>1026 Berlin, DDR

Gazetteers. Finally, a very useful tool, once your ancestors town or village is known, is the gazetteer. The most common one, which is organized according to the place names of the German Empire, is *Meyers Orts-und Verkehrslexikon des Deutschen Reiches*. This lexicon will enable you to locate the state or province in which a village is located.

Notes on Using Appendixes I and II

If you are so fortunate as to know the town or village from which your ancestor(s) came, then you may direct a query to the rectory (*Pfarramt*) in that town. If you know the state or region, then direct your query to the central church archive (either Protestant or Catholic) of that region. Your query to the local parish might well result in a reference to such an archive, anyway, since many parish records have made their way to these central repositories.

Queries about emigration and other public records should be addressed to the appropriate state archive.

Genealogical associations in various parts of Germany can be useful in providing referenced, publications, or names of professional genealogists.

Appendix I

1. Evangelical Church in Baden
   7500 Karlsruhe
   Blumenstrasse 1

2. Evangelical Church in Bavaria
   8000 Munich 2
   Meiserstrasse 13

3. Evangelical Church in Berlin-Brandenburg
   1000 Berlin 21
   Bachstrasse 1-2

4. Evangelical Lutheran Church in Brunswick (Braunschweig)
   3340 Wolfenbüttel
   Neuer Weg 88-90

5. Evangelical Church of Bremen
   2800 Bremen 1
   Franziuseck 2-4

6. Evangelical Lutheran Church of Hannover
   3000 Hannover 1
   Rote Reihe 6

7. Evangelical Church in Hesse and Nassau
   6100 Darmstadt
   Paulusplatz 1

8. Evangelical Church of Hesse:
   Electorate-Waldeck (Kurhessen Waldeck)
   3500 Kassel-Wilhelmshöhe
   Wilhelmshöher-Allee 330

9. Church of Lippe
   4930 Detmod 1
   Leopoldstrasse 27

10. Evangelical Reformed Church in Northwestern Germany
    2950 Leer
    Saarstrasse 6

11. Evangelical Lutheran Church in Oldenburg
    2900 Oldenburg
    Huntestrasse 14

12. Protestant Church of the Palatinate
    6720 Speyer
    Domplatz 5

13. Evangelical Church of the Rhineland
    4000 Düsseldorf 30
    Hans-Böcklerstrasse 7

14. Evangelical Church of Schaumburg-Lippe
    3062 Bückeburg
    Herderstrasse 27

15. Evangelical Lutheran Church in Schleswig-Holstein
    2300 Kiel 1
    Dänischestrasse 27

16. Evangelical Church of Westphalia (Westfalen)
    4800 Bielefeld 1
    Altstädter Kirchplatz 1

17. Evangelical Church in Württemberg
    7000 Stuttgart 1
    Gänseheidestrasse 2-4

Archives of the Catholic Church (according to diocese)
(West Germany)

1) *Aachen:* Generalvikariat Diözesan-Archiv
   5100 Aachen
   Klosterplatz 7

2) *Augsburg:* Ordinariat Diözesan-Archiv
   8900 Augsburg
   Fronhof 4

3) *Bamberg:* Ordinariat Diözesan-Archiv
   8600 Bamberg
   Domplatz 3

4) *Berlin:* Ordinariat Diözesan-Archiv
   1000 Berlin 19
   Wundtstrasse 48

5. *Eichstätt:* Generalvikäriat Diözesan-Archiv
   8833 Eichstätt
   Luitpoldstrasse 2

6. *Essen:* Generalvikariat Diözesan-Archiv
   4300 Essen
   Zwölfling 16

7. *Freiburg:* Ordinariat Diözesan-Archiv
   7800 Freiburg
   Herrenstrasse 35

8. *Fulda:* Generalvikariat Diözesan-Archiv
   6400 Fulda
   Paulustor 5

9. *Hildesheim:* Generalvikariat Diözesan-Archiv
   3200 Hildesheim
   Pfaffenstieg 2

10. *Köln (Cologne):* Generalvikariat Diözesan-Archiv
    5000 Koln 1
    Gereonstrasse 2-4

11. *Limburg:* Ordinariat Diözesan-Archiv
    6250 Limburg
    Rossmarkt 12

12. *Mainz:* Ordinariat Diözesan-Archiv
    6500 Mainz
    Grebenstrasse 12

13. *München (Munich):* Ordinariat Diözesan-Archiv
    8000 Munich 33
    Maxburgstrasse 2

14. *Münster:* Generalvikariat Diözesan-Archiv
    4400 Münster
    Georgskommende 19

15. *Osnabrück:* Generalvikariat Diözesan-Archiv
    4500 Osnabrück
    Hasestrasse 40A

16. *Paderborn:* Generalvikariat Diözesan-Archiv
    4790 Paderborn
    Domplatz 3

17. *Passau:* Ordinariat Diözesan-Archiv
8390 Passau
Residenzplatz 8

18. *Regensburg:* Ordinariat Diözesan-Archiv
8400 Regensburg
St. Petersweg 11-13

19. *Rottenburg am Neckar:* Ordinariat Diözesan-Archiv
7407 Rottenburg 1
Postfach 9

20. *Speyer:* Ordinariat Diözesan-Archiv
6720 Speyer
Engelsgasse 1

21. *Trier:* Generalvikariat Diözesan-Archiv
5500 Trier
Jesuitenstrasse 13B

22. *Würzburg:* Ordinariat Diözesan-Archiv
8700 Würzburg
Domerschulstrasse 2

State Archives (Staatsarchive)
(*West Germany*)

1. *Baden-Württemberg:* Hauptstaatsarchiv
7000 Stuttgart 10
Konrad-Adenaürstrasse 4

2. *Bayern (Bavaria):* Hauptstaatsarchiv
8000 Munich 2
Schönfeldstrasse 5

3. *Bremen:* Staatsarchiv
2800 Bremen
Präsident Kennedy Platz 2

4. *Hamburg:* Staatsarchiv
2000 Hamburg 36
ABC Strasse 19

5. *Hessen:* Hauptstaatsarchiv
6200 Wiesbaden
Mosbacherstrasse 55

6. *Niedersachsen (Lower Saxony):* Hauptstaatsarchiv
3000 Hannover
Planckstrasse 2

7. *Nordrhein-Westfalen (North Rhine Westphalia):*
Hauptstaatsarchiv
4000 Düsseldorf
Mauerstrasse 55

8. *Rheinland-Pfalz:* Staatsarchiv
5400 Koblenz
Karmeliterstrasse 1-3

9. *Saarland:* Landesarchiv
6600 Saarbrücken
Am Ludwigsplatz 7

10. *Schleswig-Holstein:* Landesarchiv
2380 Schleswig
Schloss Gottorf

11. *Berlin (West):* Landesarchiv
1000 Berlin 12
Strasse des 17 Juni 112

Lutheran Church Archives
(East Germany)

1. Evangelische Landeskirche Anhalts
Otto Grothewohl Strasse 22
4500 Dessau

2. Archiv und Bibliothek des Evangelischen Ministeriums
5000 Erfurt

3. Evangelisch-Lutherische Landeskirche Mecklenburgs
2761 Schwerin
Münzstrasse 8

4. Pommersche Evangelische Kirche
2200 Greifswald
Bahnhofstrasse 35

5. Evangelisch-Lutherische Landeskirche Sachsen
8032 Dresden
Lukas Strasse 6

6. Evangelische Kirche der Kirchenprovinz Sachsen
   3010 Magdeburg
   Am Dom 2

7. Evangelische Kirche von Sachsen
   8900 Görlitz
   Berlinerstrasse 62

8. Evangelische-Lutherische Kirche in Thüringen (Thuringia)
   5900 Eisenach
   Stadtparkstrasse 2

Catholic Church Archives (by bishoprics)
(*East Germany*)

1. *Berlin:* Bischöfliches Ordinariat Berlin
   1080 Berlin
   Hinter der Katholischen Kirche 3

2. *Dresden-Meissen:* Bistum Dresden-Meissen
   8057 Dresden
   Dresdenerstrasse 66

3. *Erfurt-Meiningen:* Bischöfliches Amt Erfurt-Meiningen
   5010 Erfurt
   Hermannsplatz 9

4. *Görlitz:* Apostolische Administratur
   8900 Görlitz
   Carl von Ossietzky Strasse 41

5. *Magdeburg:* Bischöfliches Amt Magdeburg
   3000 Magdeburg
   Max-Josef-Metzger-Strasse 1

6. *Schwerin:* Bischöfliches Amt Schwerin
   2761 Schwerin
   Lankower Strasse 14/16

State Archives (Item 3 is a very important archive for genealogical collections, generally.)
(East Germany)

1. Deutsches Zentralarchiv, Historische Abteilung 1
   1500 Potsdam
   Berlinerstrasse 98

2. Deutsches Zentralarchiv, Historische Abteilung II
   4200 Merseburg
   An der Weissen Mauer 48

3. Staatsarchiv, Stadtarchiv Leipzig
   7010 Leipzig
   Georgi-Dimitroff-Platz 1

Appendix II

10. *Schleswig-Holstein:* Schleswig-Holsteinsche Gesellschaft für
    Familienforschung und Wappenkunde
    2300 Kiel
    Gartenstrasse 12

11. *Berlin (West):* Verein zur Förderung der Zentralstelle für
    Personen-und Familiengeschichte
    1000 Berlin-Dahlem 33
    Archivstrasse 12-14

Notes